Hmmm...™
Little Ideas With BIG Results
by Michael Angelo Caruso

Copyright© 2000 by Michael Angelo Caruso
Third edition, 2004
Published by the Edison House
Detroit, Michigan
All rights reserved.
ISBN 0-9723296-2-5

Cover & author photo by Don Kurek
Booklet design by Night Cry Graphics

*For anyone who has made life
more complicated than it really is.*

Hmmms at a Glance

Introduction 5

People are your greatest resource 6

Find something you like 8

You can never, ever change another person 10

People like to take part 12

Keep your antenna up 14

Do you believe what people say or what they do? 16

Confrontation is good 18

Be willing to *not* know 20

"You can't hurt me" 22

The sun is out every day 24

Everything begins and everything ends 26

Dear Michael Angelo 29

5 Cool Ideas 30

www.EdisonHouse.com 31

Introduction

It's been fun releasing the third edition of *Hmmm...Little Ideas With BIG Results*. These improvements are based on feedback from hundreds of people who have published the Hmmms in corporate newsletters and thousands of audience members who have provided suggestions at my speeches and seminars.

The objective of this booklet is to help you discover new aspects of these simple thoughts and to encourage you to integrate them into your life. The Hmmms deal with fundamental life concepts – rough little diamonds that can be polished into increasingly valuable gems. The opening premise is that people are your greatest resource. The second Hmmm suggests that the best way to deal with those you don't like is to find something about them that you do like.

The Hmmms will remind you that you cannot change others, but you can influence others by allowing them to participate in reward/consequence scenarios. My favorite Hmmm teaches that the signals we trade with others can be optimized if we keep our antenna up.

One of the Hmmms explains that confrontation is beneficial, but you must be willing to *not* know what is going to happen when you confront. The secret to minimizing stress is explained by the Hmmm that states, "You Can't Hurt Me." On the days that stress gets the better of you, another Hmmm reminds that the sun is out every day and that even the darkest clouds move on.

In these ways and others, the Hmmms will serve you the rest of your days.

People are your greatest resource.

In the 1920s, George Elton Mayo first did research on teams and how they work. Mayo is largely credited for founding the modern day Human Resource department, which was then referred to as Human Relations. Mayo was a terrific speaker, but his real contribution was showing managers how to learn from employees by listening and observing. He even initiated a radical business practice called the coffee break. Supervisors of the day vehemently opposed the concept because they thought it reduced productivity.

By conducting thousands of interviews on behalf of the Western Electric Company in Chicago, Mayo learned a lot about what is expected from teams. Synergy is certainly an anticipated by-product of teams. If you've ever worked in a group, you know that you can get more done when working with others because other people usually offer something that you don't.

Women offer something different than men. Older workers offer something called "institutional memory" or a memory of how things used to be. Many new workers offer a youthful zeal. Different ethnicities and backgrounds can make a team more productive than a solo effort. It's interesting that most of us become teammates with people with whom we have something in common. We psychologically move toward people who are like us. The inverse is also true in that we psychologically move away from people with whom we have nothing in common. This "moving away" attitude can seriously diminish the value of our greatest resource.

For example, if you know 100 people and genuinely like 50 of them, you are predisposed to accessing only 50 percent of the people available to you. You've devalued your greatest resource by half. Worse still, if you regard the remaining 50 percent of the people as unfriendly, lazy or otherwise problematic, these individuals are more likely to be difficult for you later. Effective, productive people know that everyone is a great resource. Find ways to move toward all people – even people you don't like.

Find something you like about people you don't like.

If we are to nurture relationships and regard people as our greatest resource, it is helpful to find something positive about every person and build the relationship around that attribute. The truth is that everyone offers something, even if that person is "talent free." A person who is free of talent might offer us an opportunity to teach them. Maybe they offer an example of how not to be. Challenge yourself to find a redeeming quality in everyone, including people that you don't like. The fastest way to build rapport with others is to deliver a series of deep compliments.

Shallow, drive-by compliments serve a purpose, but comments like "That sweater looks good on you" and "I like your haircut" don't convey the powerful message of deep compliments. While shallow compliments involve the outside of the person's body, deep compliments involve the person's inner qualities, such as their integrity and character.

Men, in particular, sometimes struggle with delivering and accepting deep emotional compliments. A deep compliment scenario might have one man saying to another, "Jeff, I've worked with you for nearly three years. I appreciate the fact that you have never been late for anything. You have a terrific quality and I wish I had more of it. I'm glad we work together."

Our goal should be to focus on what the other person offers rather than what they lack. When you identify another person's special qualities and directly acknowledge that uniqueness, you will be practicing the real meaning of "attractiveness," thus helping your greatest resource to find you appealing. Most of us know the connotation of attractive to be young, sexy and pretty. The denotation or real meaning of being attractive, however, is the art of helping your greatest resource psychologically move closer to you. Finding something you like in others helps you focus on changing your attitude, rather than changing the other person.

You can never, ever change another person.

You cannot change another person any more than you can change the weather. Yet, humans invest large amounts of time and energy trying to change the attitude and behavior of others. Once during a seminar, I asked members of the audience if anyone had ever changed them. I was not expecting anyone to say, "Yes."

A gentleman raised his hand. In a quiet voice, he said, "I believe the Lord changed me." The crowd was hushed as they waited for my response.

"With all due respect, sir, I believe the Lord showed you how to change," I said. "Then *you* did the changing." The man slowly nodded in agreement.

It works the same way with mortals. You cannot change people. Complaining doesn't work. Gary Zukav, author of *Seat of the Soul*, reminds us that complaining is actually a form of manipulation. We often use complaints to force people to change in order to accommodate us. When the other person figures out that they are being manipulated, they feel resentment and anger. Rather than complain, a better way to solve problems is to take personal responsibility for the issue and adjust your own attitude and behavior. *Not complaining, therefore, is a form of empowerment that allows you to solve problems with or without others' compliance.*

We can't change people, but we can sometimes influence them through motivation. Sigmund Freud taught us that two things motivate people to change: the anticipation of pleasure and the avoidance of pain. When a reward/consequence scenario is clearly articulated, most people will make the right decision.

Managers, educators, spouses and parents would do well to present people with a reward/consequence scenario and let them participate by making decisions for themselves.

People don't like to take orders, they like to take part.

A manager named Sue paged an employee named Carl to her office. "Carl," she began. "I have a problem. As you know, our department recently conducted a time study to determine how we can optimize production. Carl, the results of that report show that you're producing well below the individual standard for our team."

"Since we've previously discussed how little time you spend at your desk, I have a proposal for you. Carl, let's meet again in two weeks. If your production is up to standard, I'll know that you didn't need my help. If, however, your work isn't up to standard in two weeks, I'll know that you'd be willing to move your desk next to mine so that we can work more closely together. Carl, I'll be happy with whatever you decide."

The last sentence is key because people don't like to take orders. They like to take part. In the above scenario, the clever manager psychologically helps Carl move toward an acceptable level of production. She begins with an "I statement" that Carl cannot deny, i.e., "Carl, *I* have a problem." Sue then presents evidence of the sub-standard performance. The evidence is the "report" and she uses the report to justify her reward/consequence proposal. Both of the proposal options move Carl toward Sue's desired goal and Sue pledges to support whatever decision Carl makes.

Telling people what to do may be efficient, but it's not much fun for the other person. That's why command-and-control management can be as unfulfilling as e-mail, voice mail and pagers. One-way communication saves time, but one-way signals deprive people of the opportunity for interpersonal communication.

We must learn to balance one-way communication with participative, interpersonal conversation. When we encourage participation, we will reap the full benefits of our most important dialogue.

[For a complimentary copy of the essay, "The Perils of One-Way Communication," send an e-mail (I know, I know) to PerilsofOneWayComm@EdisonHouse.com.]

When you allow others to participate, more communication signals will be available. By processing those signals, you can enrich relationships with everyone from your brother to your broker.

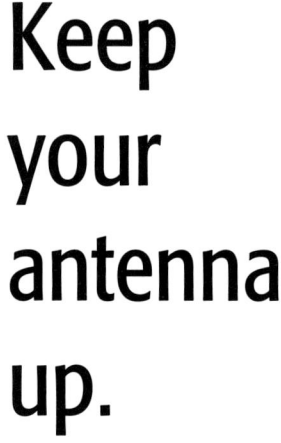

Keep your antenna up.

The secret to getting along with others is to help people feel good about themselves. People tend to feel good when they are rewarded through validation and recognition.

Metaphorically speaking, good communicators keep their antenna up in order to gain clues about how people like to be rewarded. If you are to be focused on others, it will be important to not be preoccupied with yourself. Dr. Steve Fabick, a clinical psychologist, says, "Self-consciousness can spoil even the most pleasant experience." Self-absorption certainly hampers the observation skills necessary to process other people's signals.

Behavioral psychologists use neuro-linguistic programming (NLP) to interpret non-verbal cues known as body language. Through the years, psychologists have used patterned behavior to catalog an assortment of non-verbal cues, including eye movement. For example, when a person consistently looks up and to their left while talking with you, they are likely to be accessing what experts call eidetic images. In other words, the person is probably trying to recall details of something that happened. When the person's eyes consistently move up and to their right, however, it can mean that the person is accessing constructed images. They could be hedging the truth or even lying.

[For a free chart that explains the six areas of eye movement, e-mail the author at NLPCues@EdisonHouse.com.]

Men who keep their hands in their pockets and women who walk around with their arms crossed send signals that they may be self-conscious or insecure. When your antenna is up, you will receive these signals and use the information to better understand the other person.

Of course, you are always sending signals, too. Are your non-verbal signals consistent with what you say? If not, you are displaying incongruity, which can be confusing to others when they discover a discrepancy between what you say and what you do.

Do you believe what people say or what they do?

You can believe what people do *and* say, unless they say one thing and do another. It's been said that a person with "character" says what she's going to do and then actually does it, yet the world is filled with bosses who pledge support while they constantly leverage control. Lots of married people vow fidelity and then cheat on their spouse. Ambitious individuals continually promise that they will quit smoking or lose weight, but many of them do not.

According to polls, an overwhelming number of Americans are unhappy at work. Yet, most of them will not leave their job to work elsewhere. Can this mean that they don't mind being unhappy? Clarity lies in what these people are willing to do about their predicament.

When people send us mixed signals, it's often helpful to ask them for clarification. "You tell me one thing, but you do another. Help me understand. Which is the real you?" When we confront in a calm voice without sarcasm or drama, the person will usually provide some clarity. Sometimes this type of conversation helps motivate people to analyze themselves for the real reason behind the mixed signals.

Here's a simple example of how you can match your words to your signals. If someone tells you something interesting, make a special effort to slowly move one of your hands to the lower part of your face. This will approximate the classic "Thinker Pose" made famous by the French sculptor, Rodin. If you say something like "What you just said is very interesting," the Thinker Pose will match your verbal signal.

Attentive people will be sure to notice character gaps between what is being said and what is being done. In any case, signal incongruity can result in hurt feelings, misunderstandings and negative energy. When these things occur, confrontation skills can be very useful.

Confrontation is good.

An infected cut on your hand usually requires special attention in the form of an antibiotic. Confrontation is the antibiotic for a troubled relationship. Confrontation is a healing agent because it can force two people to resolve an issue.

Fear of confrontation has led many individuals to settle for a compromised ideal. People who practice conflict avoidance are likely to experience negative consequence and less likely to get what they want. Conversely, a person who practices skillful confrontation is likely to be rewarded for their effort. Purposeful, skillful confrontation is good.

When my father was dying, doctors suggested transitioning him to hospice, but my brothers and I didn't want Dad to think that we were giving up on him. The family hoped Dad would make the hospice decision himself. In a quiet moment, I asked my father a very confrontational question. "Dad, are you going to get better?" When my father answered, "I think I'm improving," we decided not to mention hospice to him. He died 36 hours later. The confrontational exchange allowed our family members to trade more signals, which helped us collect more information. Thanks to that new information, Dad died in a positive frame of mind.

[Hear the complete story on the audiobook, *Dear Michael Angelo – A Father's Life Letters to His Son*, which is available at www.EdisonHouse.com.]

It's been said that there are three types of people in the world: aggressive, assertive and passive. Assertive people engage in purposeful, strategic confrontation. They get what they want and don't take advantage of others. Aggressive people get what they want by taking advantage of others, burning bridges almost as fast as they can build them. Passive people who practice conflict avoidance, usually don't get what they want.

Sometimes even assertive people are uncomfortable with confrontation because conflict stirs emotions. Emotions are sometimes unsettling and uncertain. Yet, to achieve purposeful confrontation, you must be willing to *not* know what is going to happen.

Be willing
to *not* know
what is
going
to happen.

Comfort level is important because it drives conventional decision-making. When people are comfortable they are usually more confident. When confident, people are more decisive. And when people are more decisive, they are more comfortable. But, your propensity for cycling through the comfortable-confident-decisive-comfortable sequence is not exclusively determined by your need to feel emotionally safe. Indeed, newness in your life is also regulated by your willingness to be *un*comfortable.

Most of us are reluctant to try something new unless we are guaranteed a desirable outcome. Alas, life is filled with unforeseeable, uncontrollable and unavoidable scenarios. Under these conditions, it is okay to *not* know what is going to happen.

In the middle of my first rock climbing experience, I suddenly became too anxious to descend. I had rehearsed the rappel technique prior to climbing the rock face but the practice did little to alleviate my discomfort. Rappelling requires the climber to hold the safety rope, lean backward into space and prop the bottoms of his or her feet against the vertical surface. I'm told that experienced climbers actually enjoy rappelling.

Uncomfortable with the limitations of my climbing ability, I was not confident in my decision to descend and suffered a brief, but paralyzing anxiety attack. This, of course, made me even more uncomfortable. Unsure and untrusting, I lingered at the top of the rock face until I was willing to *not* know what was going to happen. Then, I leaned backward and climbed down.

When you don't know what is going to happen, try to anticipate positive results. The coolest people I know are comfortable even when they are uncomfortable. What will happen when you are patient enough to find something that you like about people you don't like? What will happen when you endure the discomfort of confronting a bothersome person? How will you feel when you are stress-free and no one can hurt you?

◆ ◆ ◆

"You can't hurt me."

If you want a low-stress life, you must learn to refuse delivery on negativity. Refusing to sign for stress packages requires personal power that comes from living these four words: "You can't hurt me."

The advanced version of "You can't hurt me" is "You won't hurt me, I trust you not to hurt me."

"You can't hurt me" is a style. People with this style are happy almost all the time. Free from perceived threats and unwelcome influence, "you can't hurt me" people are carefree and seem to get along with everyone. They are assertive rather than aggressive and have no need to change people. They allow others to participate in communication and decision-making. People who practice "you can't hurt me" embrace confrontation as a technique to improve relations. Independent and fulfilled, they find a sense of adventure and wonder in every encounter. Optimistic and upbeat, people with a "you can't hurt me" philosophy feel good mentally and physically.

You can develop a "you can't hurt me" cachet because you can learn new attitudes and behavior. The psychologist Piaget believed that we spend much of life unlearning things we have been taught. Perhaps you have been taught that people can hurt you and now you need to unlearn it. Philosopher John Locke wrote that we are all born a white slate or *tabula rasa*. Mommy, Daddy, aunts and uncles, siblings, friends and teachers write on the slate when we are young and we have trouble erasing some of that writing.

Here are ways that you can rewrite your slate. The "you can't hurt me" attitude is conveyed through a sophisticated series of signals like how you walk into a room, where you sit in the room, how you present yourself, the non-verbal communication you send and the words you use. You can learn to stop harming yourself with your own words and actions by replacing those messages with signals that convey, "you can't hurt me."

"You can't hurt me" is a powerful creed because it plays to your strength. You have no control over others, but you have complete control over *your reaction to them*. Who wants to be human Velcro for negativity and worry? Stop leaving the "welcome mat" out for stress and every day will be a good day.

The sun is out every day.

Professional development will help you manage problems at work. Communication skills will enrich the quality of your personal relationships. A good attitude will take the edge off most bad scenarios. But let's face it, some dark days will have you repeating the famous Dorothy Parker line: "What fresh hell is this?"

I boarded the airplane, although it was not a good day to be flying. I could hear the fierce rain pelting the roof of the metal tube as I took my seat. Powerful winds caused the plane to sway and we weren't even airborne yet.

Seated, I couldn't see six inches past the window. The scene was eerie and foreboding. A fog had enveloped the aircraft. We would be flying by radar. A red light pulsed somewhere on the wing as the plane lumbered down the runway. We gained ground speed and took flight into the murky, soupy air.

The red light on the wing continued to pulse through the fog. The plane continued its ascent, lunging and jerking upward. Finding its way, the aircraft shimmied as it climbed higher and higher. The ride gradually became smoother as we gained altitude, climbing, climbing, until we cruised into bright, pristine sunshine.

This is possible because the sun is out every day.

The question is: "Are you going to fly your plane in the clouds or above them?" Know that overcast skies can hide the sun, but *undercast* skies won't bother you much.

On really bad days, try to recall good things that have happened for you. Then, focus on positive things that you know are about to happen. When you preoccupy your mind with fond thoughts of recent accomplishments and the anticipation of more good stuff, the "ugly" present is much more bearable.

On cloudy days, take solace in knowing that everything begins and everything ends. Remember, clouds move.

Everything begins and everything ends.

Like clouds, friends, drift in and out of our lives. Jobs begin and end. Possessions get lost and sometimes stolen. We should learn to relax ourselves to the ebb and flow of life. Imposing our will on the universe, only perpetuates our anxiety and lack of fulfillment.

Two of my brothers once worked for a small computer company. One of the company's new technicians had to be let go because he wasn't right for the job. The day after he was fired, a pizza was delivered to the office. Attached was a note from the person they had fired. The note read, "Thank you very much for the opportunity to work with your company. I'm sorry I had to leave, but I learned a lot during our short time together and I wish you all success."

Nobody ate the pizza.

Assuming the pizza wasn't poisonous, I think the fired employee had the right idea. Jobs come and go. Knowing this, why do we insist on tortuous transitions and melodramatic exits? Certainly, emotions play a role. Jealousy, anger, pride, avarice and envy tug at our ego, distracting us from the intractable conclusion. Everything begins and everything ends.

If this fact is so obvious, why do we struggle? We struggle because emotion cripples rational thought. Whenever your emotions are pulling you in uncomfortable directions, go with them for a little while. Then, push the reset button. Allow yourself to center on life's simple ideas and take action as though the quality of your life depends on it. Know that people are your greatest resource. Focus on what you *like* about people. Remember that you can never, ever change another person. Let others take part.

Keep your antenna up. Believe what people do rather than what they say. Understand that confrontation is good. Be willing to *not* know what is going to happen. Practice "You can't hurt me" and you can cultivate personal power. Remember the sun is out every day. Be aware that everything begins and everything ends.

The unofficial camping motto urges us to focus on what's really important: Leaving the place better than we found it. This allows others to benefit from our experience. After all, we are other people's greatest resource. *Hmmm...*

Dear Michael Angelo
A Father's Life Letters to His Son
An audiobook by Michael Angelo Caruso, read by the author

My dad, Mickey Caruso, wrote over fifty letters between 1993 and 1997. These missives include dozens of vignettes that tell how his parents immigrated to the United States, what it was like to grow up during the Depression, how music impacted his life and what it was like to grow up with eleven brothers and sisters. These letters became a retroactive diary that chronicled the best of his life and taught me the value of keeping a journal to document life changes.

In the summer of 1997, my Dad and I talked about publishing his letters, but on September 24, our family changed again. As another chapter played out, the value of the written word became apparent…and yet another lesson was handed down from my father. Dad and I missed our opportunity to work together on this project, but my brothers and I know that he would want you to enjoy the world according to Mick. Dad's letters were a method of passing the benefits of his life lessons on to his family. With each person who experiences these letters, Mickey's family grows.

What people are saying:

"*I listened to* Dear Michael Angelo *twice before I figured out that the letters are not about Michael and his Dad as much as they are about my Dad and me.*"
– Brenda Geist, Ft. Belvoir, VA

"*I listened to stories from Michael's Dad and immediately wrote to my sons.*"
– Marty Bostrom, Marysville, TN

"*… stirred my soul. I've given it to my children to urge them to keep their communication and love open.*"
– Lou Seimer, Baltimore, MD

5 Cool Ideas
For Better Working, Living & Feeling
By Michael Angelo Caruso

5 Cool Ideas on over 60 topics, including better speaking and listening, saving money, increasing motivation, staying healthy, better writing, reducing stress, better sleep, remembering names, losing headaches and dealing with difficult people.

For many years, I have kept a log of my useful ideas.

Categorized by topic and easily digested in groups of five, I call each packet "5 Cool Ideas." As time went on and my consulting business grew, the idea catalog became more comprehensive. I mailed them to friends, family and clients. They were published in various newsletters and newspapers. Feedback was extraordinary.

I have included some of the ideas in my company's website at www.EdisonHouse.com where visitors can enter the kitchen of my cyber house and look in the fridge for "Cool Ideas." My brother, Dave, gets credit for that brilliant idea.

This book is a collection of my "5 Cool Ideas." Inside, you'll find "5 Cool Ideas" for reducing stress, getting good sleep and networking. There are "5 Cool Ideas" for safe travel, being happier and making more money. You will benefit from over 20 topics and more than 100 killer ideas.

I hope my cool ideas help you develop your cool ideas.

What people are saying:

"'Smiling through doorways' is the best idea I've learned in years! It gives me new confidence and keeps other people guessing."
– Jim Rennie, Tucson, AZ

"I love the 'Most Important Words' you can use with another person."
– Stephanie Holte, Minneapolis, MN

"Love the '5 Cool Ideas for Creating Personal Power.' My difficult people have been put on notice and my life is better every day!"
– Kenneth Bateman, Newark, NJ

Highlights from www.EdisonHouse.com

MichaelCaruso@EdisonHouse.com
Books, Tapes & CDs | Calendar | Programs | Cool Ideas™ | Michael In Print
Rave Reviews | Guest Book | Contact Us

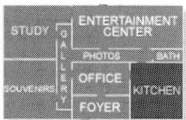

Michael's Calendar

Sunday	Monday	Tuesday	Wednesday	Thursday	Friday	Saturday
	Creativity Camp, Boston	Hero School, New York	Hmmm, DC	Talk to Me, Richmond	Talk to Me, Raleigh	

Programs

- How to Deal with Difficult People
- Secrets to Proactive Communication
- Personal Power: The Art of Being More Attractive
- Thinking on Your Feet
- Sales Workshop (Advanced)
- Hero School for Managers

Gallery

Here, you can have fun with the people and events that have helped shape my life. Click on any picture to read the stories behind the images.

Michael Angelo Caruso In Print

Books – Newspapers – Magazines

Rooms: Home | Office | Souvenirs | Kitchen | Entertainment Center | Study | Gallery | Floor Plan
Subjects: Books, Tapes, CDs | Calendar | Programs | Cool Ideas™ | Michael in Print | Rave Reviews | Guestbook | Contact Us